carry the sky

for us

— dedication

pain is only beautiful
in poetry

do not let it trick you
into thinking
otherwise

— foreword

we
carry
the
sky

mckayla
robbin

part i

mckayla robbin

the women in
my family
carry
in our bones
the sky

all women carry
the sky
inside of them
didn't your mother
ever
tell you that

the same blood coursing through your veins
also coursed
through your mother's veins
and her mother's and her mother's mother's and
back and back
since the beginning of time

what ancient magic is this

mckayla robbin

we have pasts
rattling through us
that refuse
to stay buried

pardon me i have my own history to unearth

— feminine

sorry to be a woman,
eve learned to say
and
now we have to
unteach
her apology
from our
mouths

mckayla robbin

how long has the blame
rested
squarely
on our shoulders

i am setting it down now

i have other clouds
to carry

and how many times do we chew up
our words
swallow our tongues
claw off our throats
out of loyalty to the people who
least deserve our allegiance

there will always be the chapter
you wish you didn't have to write

— the heroine dies in this one

my body opens
into ghosts
who turn around me like the night
and come from places
i don't like to remember the names of

no one knows how to say
the things
we should never have had
to learn:

how, suddenly,
what cannot be taken away
is taken

— sexual assault

she paints a door on the wall
of her mind
steps through it
and
disappears

— aftermath

if i cannot feel safe
in my own skin
there is no corner of this earth
warm enough

mckayla robbin

indivisible with liberty and justice for all
when i tell of my country it is not yet this version

a question you should never
have to ask
just for walking out your door
wearing
the color of your skin

— will i live

mckayla robbin

in orlando charlotte charleston ferguson

that was my child and that was my brother and
that was my sister and that was my mother and

how many more

mckayla robbin

i am tired
even history says so, closing her eyes

together we move.
one foot
in
front of the other.
stomping up the mountain.
hauling
the whole earth.

— progress

anger walks on one side of me.
love on the other.

i have seen women
wrap
their lives
quietly
in parentheses
while men take over
whole countries
with their fists

do you want these ten thousand ships
this war
she imagines him asking
every night
as they brush their teeth before bed

call it off
call it off
call it off

— helen of troy

.

if i was too drunk
to consent
why do i still
hesitate
to call it
what it was

— rape culture

her mouth is a graveyard
full
of all the words
fear
has drowned

mckayla robbin

afterwards what's gone
is
a common language
sifting
through the river
searching for
syllables
that fit your tongue

mckayla robbin

it is pronounced like loss
it is pronounced like broken glass
it is pronounced like trying
to gather yourself
back into your body

it's okay to let the pain
keep you
for a little while.

to stand in the rain with it.

hold its hand.

mckayla robbin

even cleopatra was sometimes
just a human
weeping in her bedroom
begging for another queen
to lift
her burden[1]

---

[1] *after 'pain' by ijeoma umebinyuo*

in her dreams she shouts
woman woman
who am i
woman

i cannot hold me steady.

this sky
leaking
through
my fingers.

these clouds
pinning
me to the bed.

like a star,
the light you carry
lives on
without you

knowing this
did not
make it any easier
to lose you

— for marigene

and of the countless wounds
the earth has worn
this one
is one too many to bear

no use shaking
the world
and hoping
a reason
will
fall out

yet here i again am
turning
every ocean
upside down

— tragedy

mckayla robbin

sorrow is not rain, it cannot
dry up
from one bright morning

in us,
ten thousand years of it
well up

mckayla robbin

mother how have we not grown tired
of holding our spines
upright
all of these years

part ii

mckayla robbin

i am washing the sky
how else can i
make sense
of all this blood

america
when will you
stop
unmothering
your people

— motherland

mckayla robbin

do not ask what your country can do for you
ask
if your country carries hate
inside her
if hate is walking down her spine,
possessing her cities

the defensiveness you hold on your tongue
is bitter
what i am asking for is sweetness
is honey
instead

mckayla robbin

even after all this evolving
it seems we
still only know how
to speak in fists

take off your skin
walk up someone else's staircase

— put yourself in the way of diversity

audre lorde.
lucille clifton.
chimamanda ngozi adichie.
rupi kaur.
nayyirah waheed.
yrsa daley-ward.
ijeoma umebinyuo.
warsan shire.
sonia sanchez.

— bookshelf

straighten your shoulders
and turn your palms
upwards
this is how we have
carried the sky
for generations

see how the body
becomes
a mouth

— true activism

mckayla robbin

susan b. anthony last time i saw you
we were waiting for her
on the corner of pennsylvania ave
and then one hundred years
interrupted
our conversation[1]
and
she must be coming anytime now
anytime now

— madame president

<hr>

[1] *after 'to merle' by lucille clifton*

mckayla robbin

someday

— a prayer

to every woman who
unbuttons
her human light
and grows like a vine
wherever
they don't want her

your resilience
has lifted
nations

— a toast

her strength
has been
scorned
vilified
sentenced to death
for centuries

— night is a woman

forget everything you learned before

your body
is not a war
it is a celebration

mckayla robbin

i am queen of
my country my home my body
my country my home my body
my country my home my body

why is this even up for discussion

how can i shed this snakeskin
this anger rooted into my scalp
when it is the only thing
preventing me
from turning to stone

— medusa

mckayla robbin

listen to the moon: she has known
the earth
a long time

— wisdom

mckayla robbin

i am unfolding
my fists
and finding flowers there

i am unfolding
my fists
and finding fire there

mckayla robbin

do not confuse fire
for hatred
because
we might be burning
but only love
can raise us from these ashes

learning how to carry the sky means
learning
how to hold the sun
in one hand
and the moon in the other
strength in one hand
and softness
in the other

— balance

it's not called listening
if
you're just waiting
for your turn to speak

— a sign of privilege

mckayla robbin

no
is a necessary magic

no
draws a circle around you
with chalk
and says
i have given enough

— boundaries

beware the woman
who
emerges
from the lake

beware the woman
who
takes back her sword

— excalibur

mckayla robbin

your body is a deafening symphony
of muscles lungs and
breath
do you understand how
mesmerizing
that is

deep inside your belly
dwells
a powerful darkness
soft enough
to make
all life grow

— dark magic

mckayla robbin

to be afraid
of the dark
is
to be afraid
of your own power

— to the girl who sleeps with the light on

i am starving
for something i don't know what
a bed where i can rest
a forgiveness i haven't met yet

mckayla robbin

look at the sky goddamn look at it

— the first poem

sometimes to be here at all
despite everything
is the most i can do

even pushing air through my lungs
is
on certain days
like moving mountains

mckayla robbin

after all i have never really
felt at home
on this lonely blue planet
ruled by a species
hardly paying any
attention
to the home we are ruining
almost completely

we have to work, we all must work,
to plant trees
that will grow apples
we will never personally have a taste of

mckayla robbin

the world asks for fear
and instead
you must breathe
love into it

there is no good reason for anything
and still
i can't stop trying to
salvage
flowers from the wreckage

and after all what a privilege
hope is

pick up your hands
put them
back on your wrists
and cup them around the earth
as though around a pottery wheel
for you are not powerless
and there is work
to be done

part iii

vulnerability is water
is art
and whether a blessing or a curse i cannot say
but the most necessary thing
on the planet

mckayla robbin

come
unlace your boots
and let us be soft together
because lord knows
these years
have been hard enough already[1]

---

[1] *after p. 60 of <u>milk and honey</u> by rupi kaur*

mckayla robbin

let the ancient catastrophe begin

— the queen of hearts

i beg my body to be good
but
it is persistent with all of its
dizzying wicked magics

if it is me you want here i am

— witchcraft

longing, you know, is
unbearable
the world is too narrow for it

the room where you gave me the stars
i remember

mckayla robbin

afterwards my body is strange to itself
standing in the shower
hollowed out
from the very thing
that is supposed to make you feel whole

— not pillow talk

seven years now i have put on
your heart
and still it doesn't fit me

mckayla robbin

at the ocean i shout out
your name
hoping, perhaps,
for some semblance of you
but i know
i already know
not a single sound ever comes back
to the mouth it leaves from

heartbreak hands you a needle
without thread
and somehow you are expected
to sew

for this i recommend
you make
a standing appointment
every tuesday
at two o'clock
with a cup of tea
and a good cry

be careful of loving someone
who does not know how
to speak the language of the sky
who does not know how
to hold you
without wanting
to pull your language out of your mouth
and shove his own into it

mckayla robbin

growing up the acceptable type
of woman
was not a sudden loss
instead it was a slow seeping out
like blood
from a pricked finger

— sleeping beauty

i am trying
i think
to erase me
from myself

— eating disorder

mckayla robbin

how many days
do we spend
trying
to be smaller
than we are

someone's always hushing up
the gory bits
but what good is shame finally
it locks your heart shut

— the scarlet letter

i unbuckle my spine
and
stick an apology between
my teeth

this is how we have folded ourselves
neatly
into men's lives
for generations

the oldest story in the book

a girl taking off her body
for a boy

— cinderella's stepsister

you were her, once
and she is still inside you
cracking
the bones of your heart
like thunder

— past self

keep watch for the woman
who will rise
from the middle of you.

who will reclaim the moon.

keep watch
because
you do not yet know the day
or the hour.

— awakening

mckayla robbin

some people will always want to break you
into easy to swallow
pieces
but try as they might they cannot
tear the sky
in two

your life is not a footnote
in someone else's story

mckayla robbin

tell me how to learn
the art
of forgetting

that old waltz

eventually
the smallest part of you
an ankle perhaps
or a wrist
is the only place
this whole body hurt
will live

— give it time

mckayla robbin

and how unready you always are
for another person
to press
their palm
into the center of your heart[1]

---

[1] *after 'scar' by nayyirah waheed*

mckayla robbin

i still plant you
in lines of my poetry

mckayla robbin

it's spring i suppose so
you blossom like poppies
in the window boxes
of my mind
and i want you to know i do
miss you darling
but mostly
i'm doing just fine

i don't know if people always leave
but i am glad
you showed up
for however little or long it was
and i will never not be glad
about that

so i have found puddles of happiness
without you

me in my polka dot rainboots
hop hop hopping
along the avenue

someday it won't have to be
a revolution
for a woman to stand in a doorway
kissing
another woman

someday it won't have to be
a revolution
and it can just be
what it is

— love is love is love

when love arrives
she is
some sort of pine tree
growing
through these black hills
which is to say through
the heart
of everything that is

— after the translation of the lakota *paha sapa*

you must first become
your own shape
before you can find somebody else
to fit it

part iv

mckayla robbin

these days i am hiking
back
to myself
it's a long road
the hills lead to other hills

you can only bring with you what you have
and flowers and poems
do as much good as anything else

wherever
i go,
there
home is

— reminder

i reach for solitude
and
brush the pulse
of the entire universe

— walking in the woods

mckayla robbin

when i am old i imagine
a bench
overlooking the winter shore
will please me
obscurely

the world inhales, it is day
exhales, it is night

inhales, exhales
inhales, exhales

steadying us into the future

if you paint shut the window
over your heart
i will water the flowers
in the yard out front
so that when you are ready
you will have
something lovely
to look at

— unconditional love

mckayla robbin

thank you for pulling the sun up
over the horizon
when i was too tired
from staying up all night
holding
the stars in place

— for my best friend

the most
extraordinary
love affairs
of my life

— female friendships

i am pushing my bones back into my body

gently
gently now

mckayla robbin

since we last spoke
i have threaded my sorrow
into a sweater
and i am learning, i think,
to wear it
without letting it break me

dancing is how your soul remembers
to love
your body

mckayla robbin

and when we get to dancing
oh how it
mends us right up

i am free and spinning
as a wheel
of light
please never ask me
to say sorry
for such a thing

— my life belongs only to me

mckayla robbin

an infinite girl beneath a fixed star

so overflowing, every eyelash
stood
for something

— passion

i sew my dreams
into the soil
and pray for rain

— patience

mckayla robbin

shape your words into clouds
soft
full of water

watching someone else have
the success you want
is painful
but you have to trust
that you'll find
your own way to it

your life is the unique
and unapologetic
fingerprint
you leave
on this world

do not waste it
wishing
you had someone else's

— legacy

when my heart cracks open
stars pour out
what else can i do
except
make music out of it

mckayla robbin

tomorrow
is big
and
unopened
as the sky

follow your light
wherever
that indignant candle
leads you

mckayla robbin

there's always paris

i have grown poems
like wildflowers
from the wounds
that for years
would not close up

mckayla robbin

thank you poems for your patience

you sister are the sound
of the color of
a flower
and when they
out of their own insecurity
try to silence you
you must bloom
anyways

how can you not
see
what i see
your royal wild soul
pouring out
of your chest

it's in your bones: the day
and night
at once

every light you need
is already
inside of you

— lullaby

in a small and quiet room
sit cross-legged with your grief
let it run like a river
through you
until it has carved your spirit
into a deep canyon
that holds whole ecosystems
teeming
with new life

— healing

mckayla robbin

consider
the unfolding of your breath
and like some sort of
north star
it will show you
where to go from here

mckayla robbin

on days like today
it is enough
to tip your head towards
the sky
and forgive yourself

mckayla robbin

anyways i have
no regrets about this

mckayla robbin

fasten hope to your hair
like a ribbon
until
it catches a gust of wind
and carries you
to all the wild shores
you did not
dare
to go before

mckayla robbin

and so it always is

when you least expect it
the door opens
to even the remotest parts of stars

— never give up

let it be what it is, love:

the beginning
of everything

i want to thank
all of our
ancient nameless sisters
who straightened unflinchingly
and swore
to unsilence themselves

— acknowledgement

mckayla robbin is a writer based in charleston, south carolina. *we carry the sky* is her first book of poetry and the culmination of a summer spent writing at the jersey shore.

68540076R00089